I0476444

How To Draw Skulls Tattoos Basic Designs

Pencil Drawing Ideas for Absolute Beginners

By Gala Publication

Published By:

Gala Publication

ISBN-13: 978-1515169758
ISBN-10: 1515169758

Table of Contents

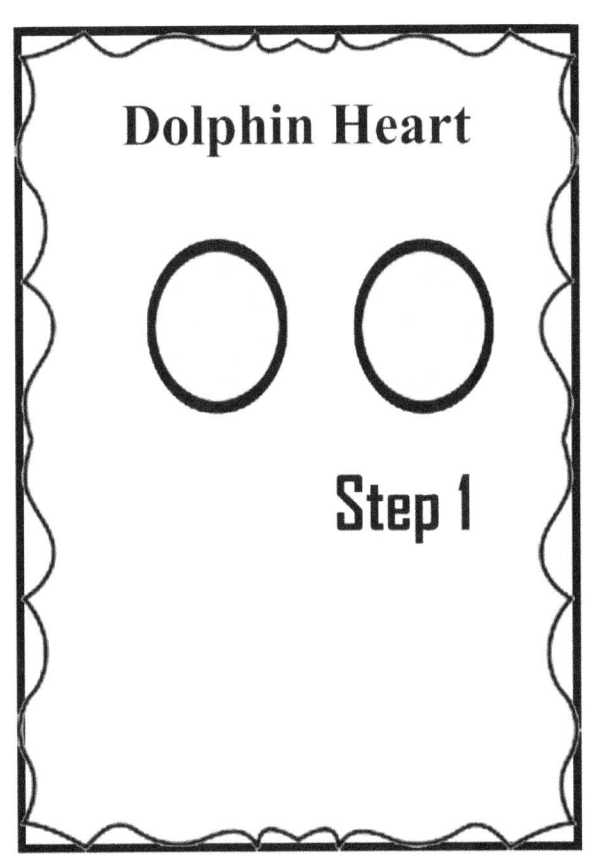

Dolphin Heart

Step 1

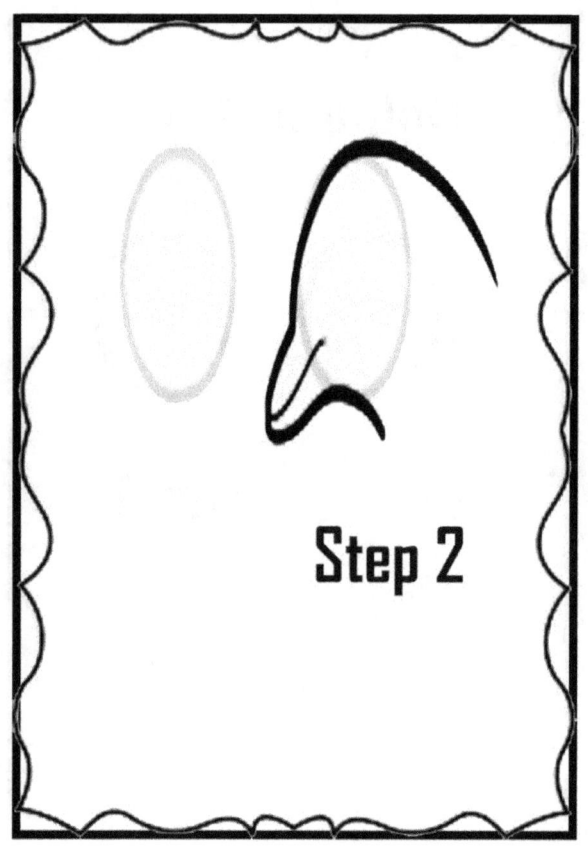

Step 2

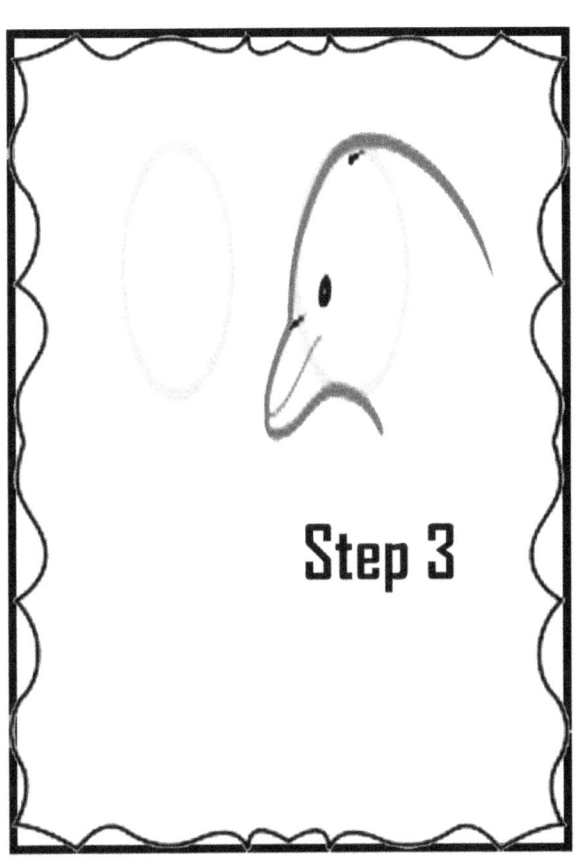

Step 3

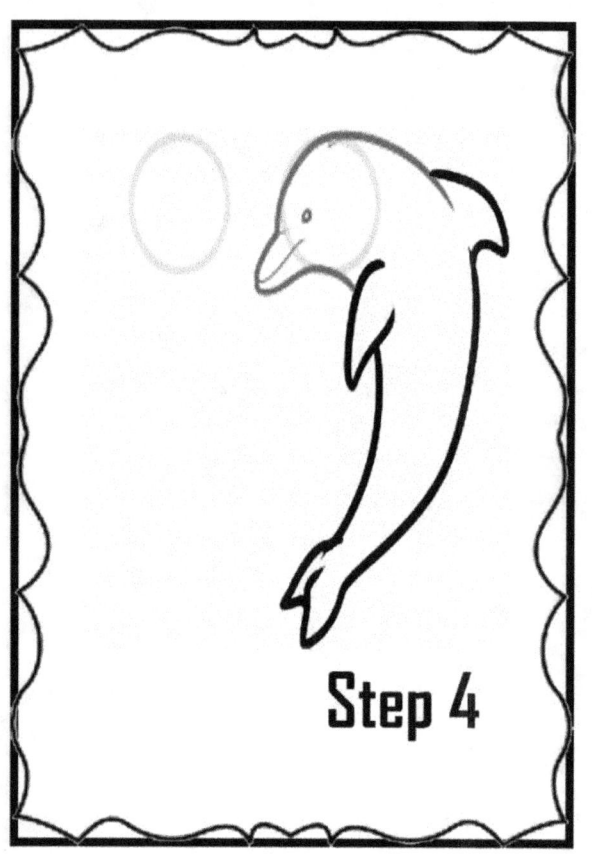

Step 4

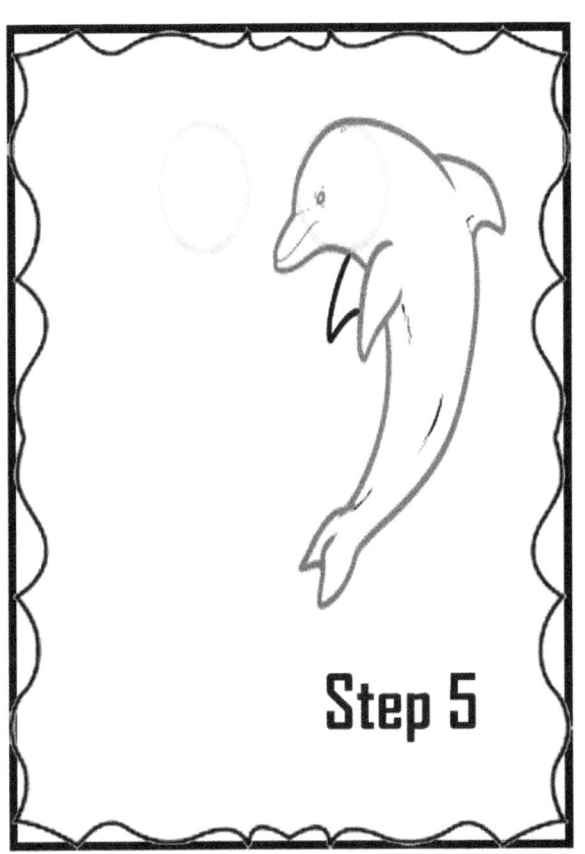

Step 5

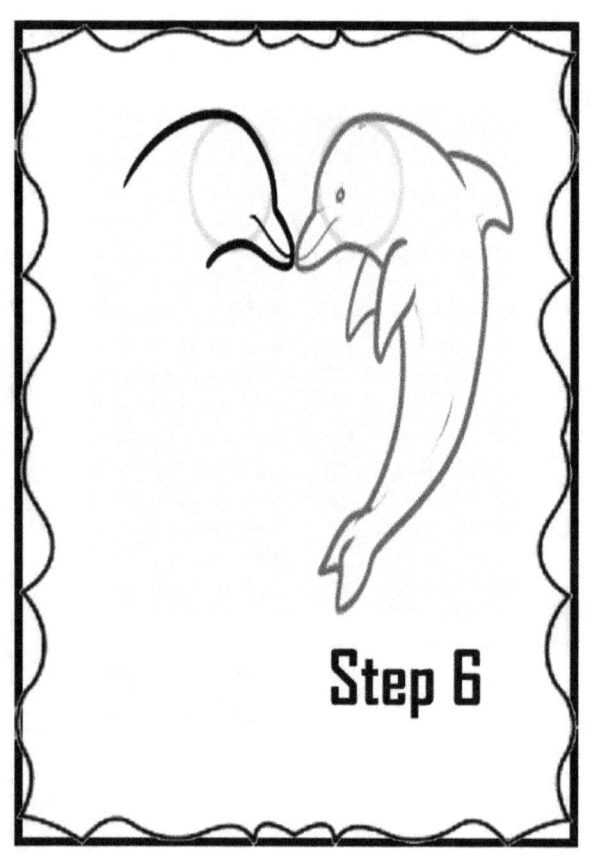

Step 6

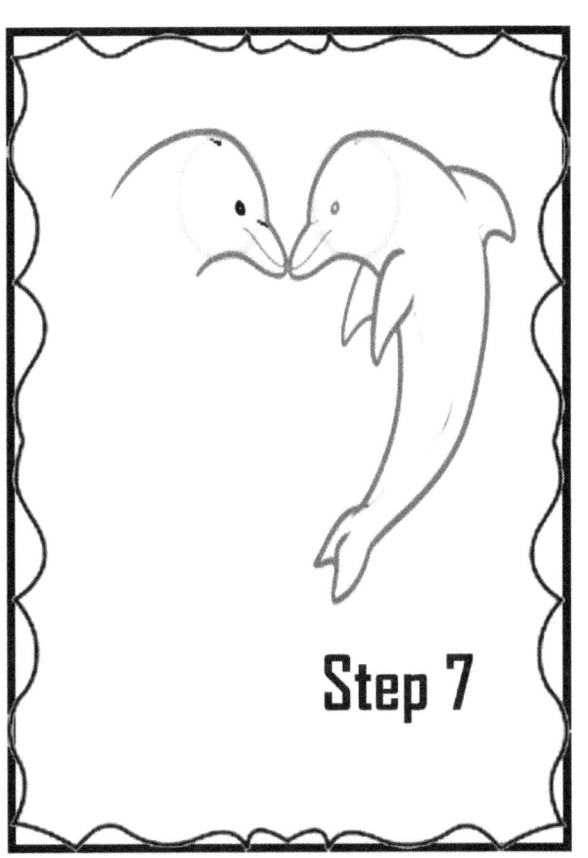

Step 7

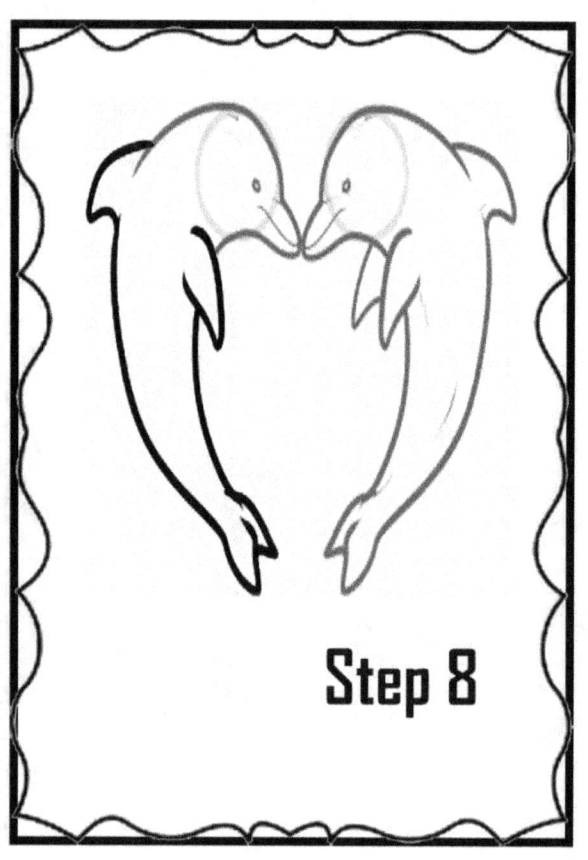

Step 8

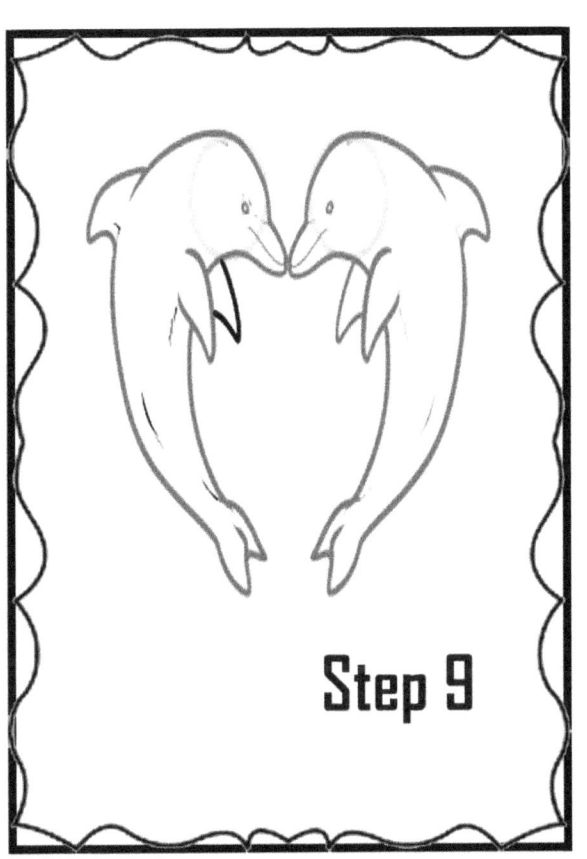

Step 9

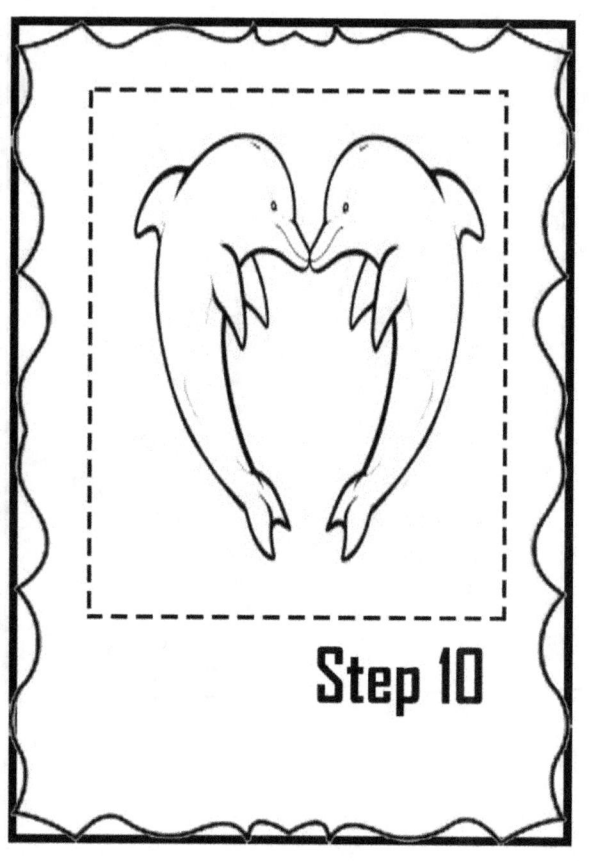

Step 10

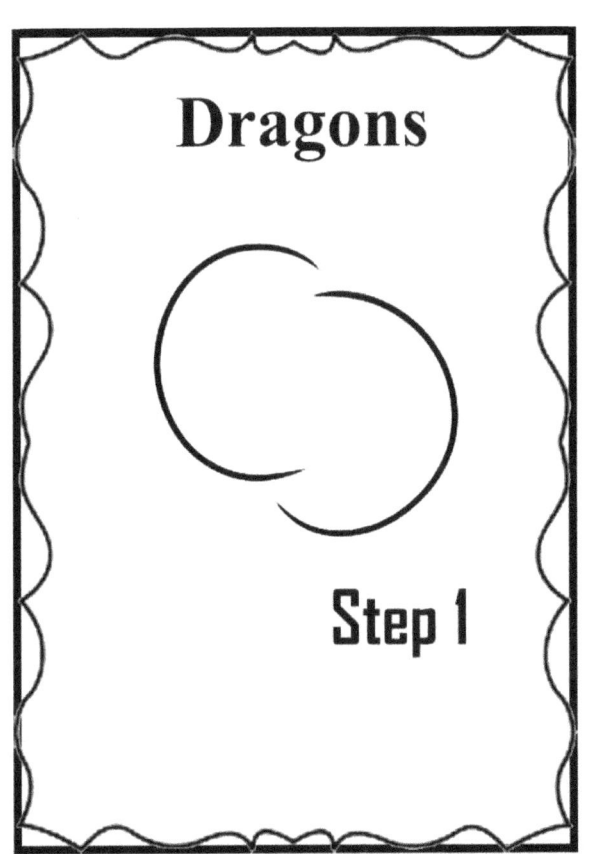

Dragons

Step 1

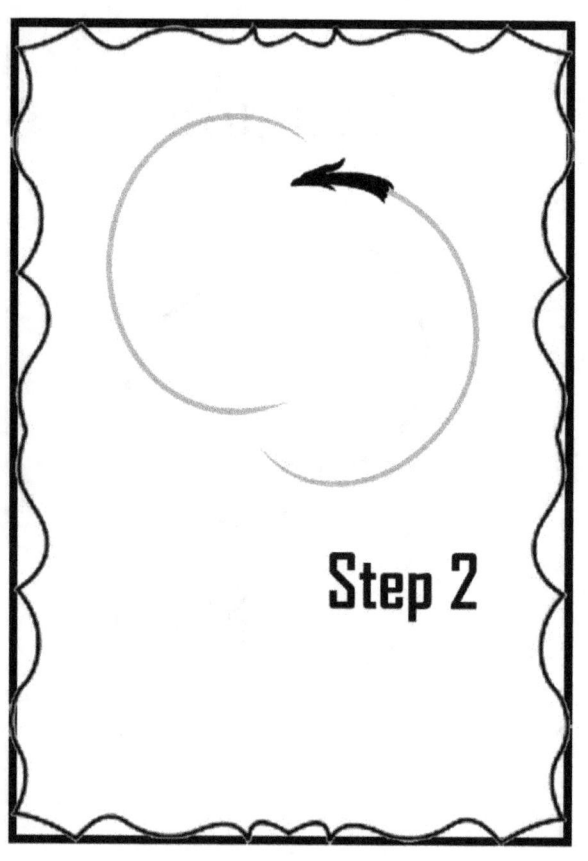

Step 2

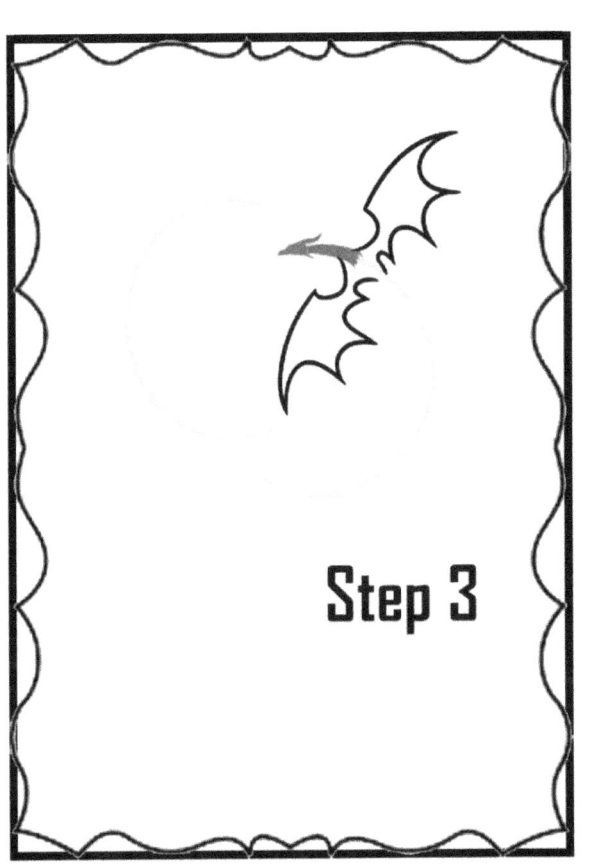

Step 3

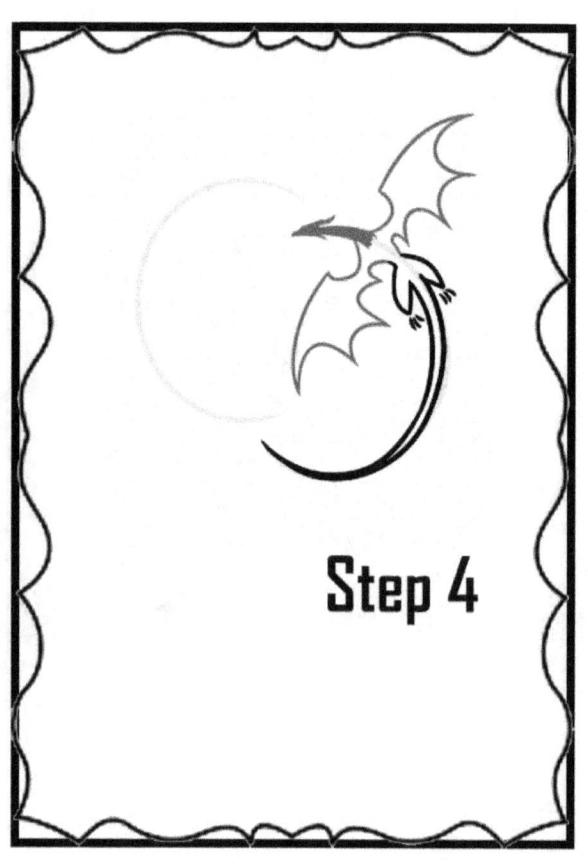

Step 4

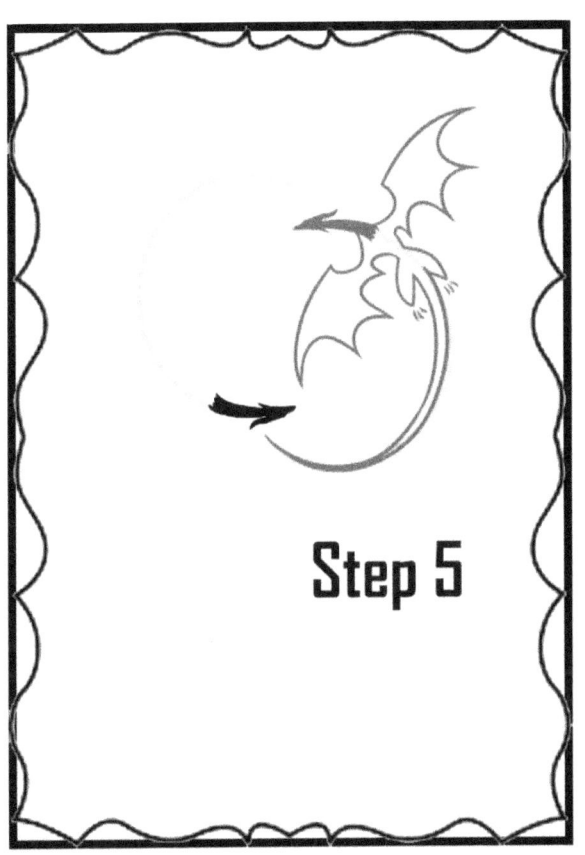

Step 5

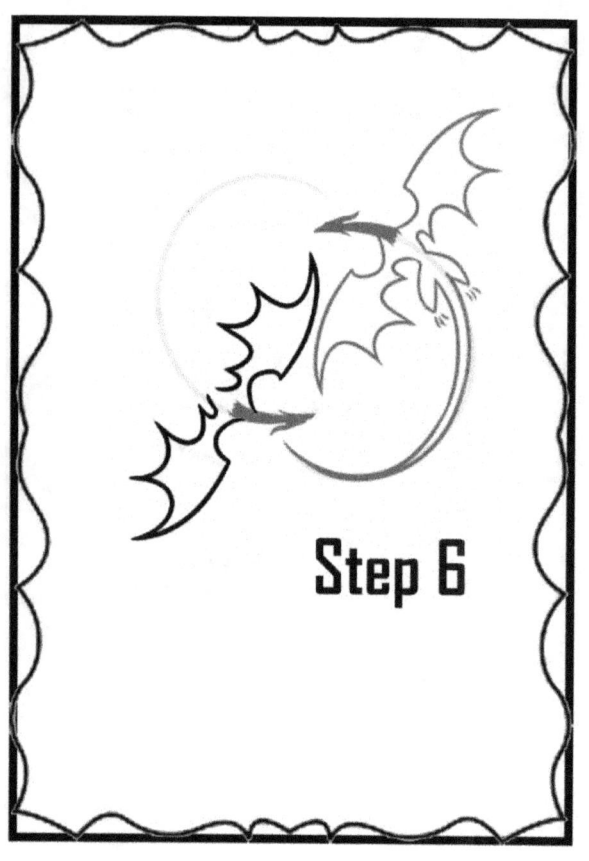

Step 6

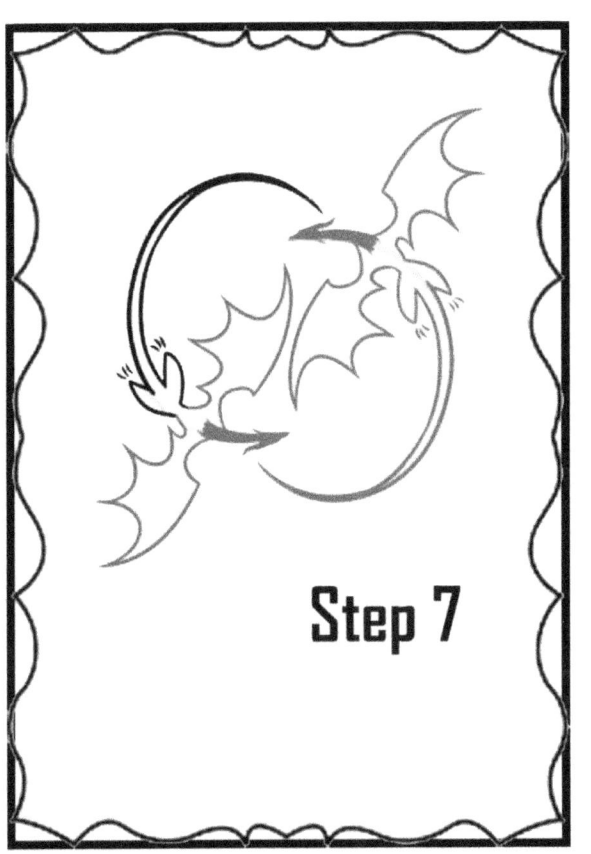

Step 7

Step 8

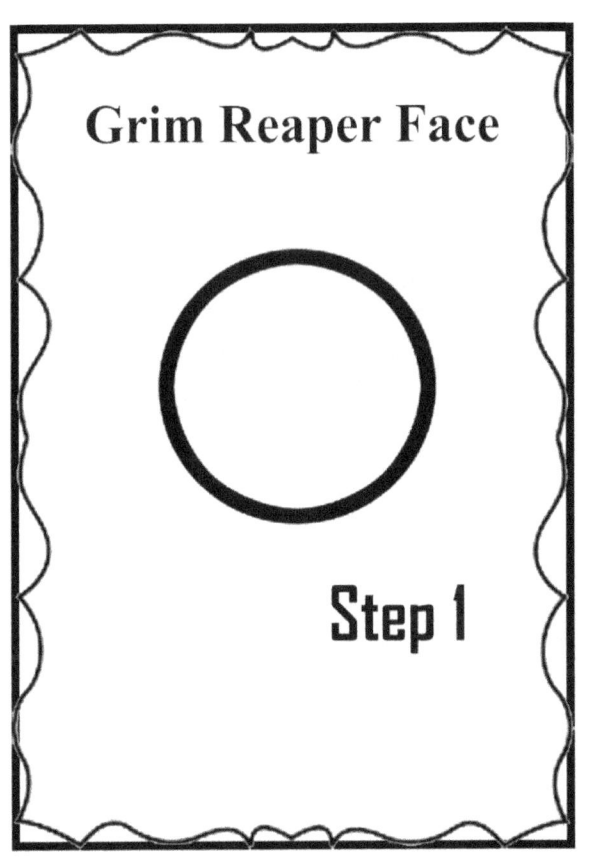

Grim Reaper Face

Step 1

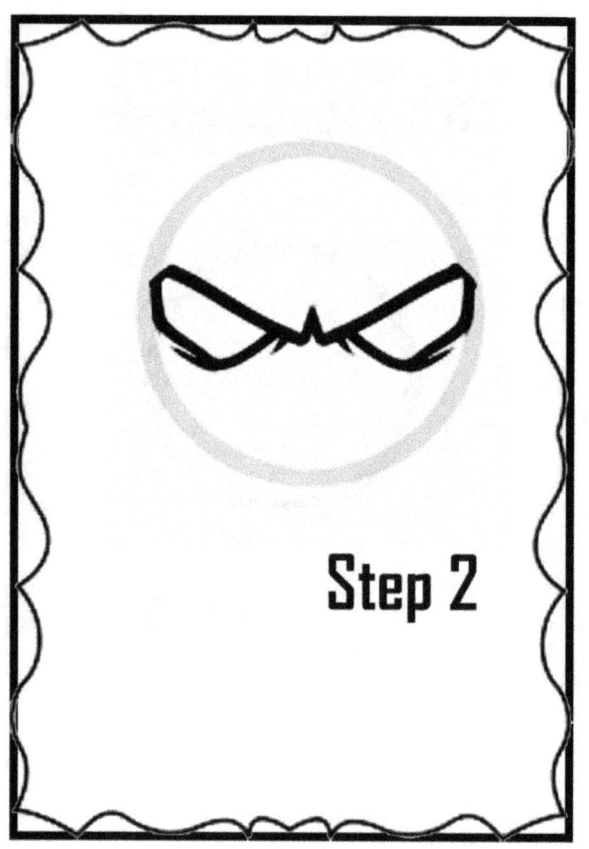

Step 2

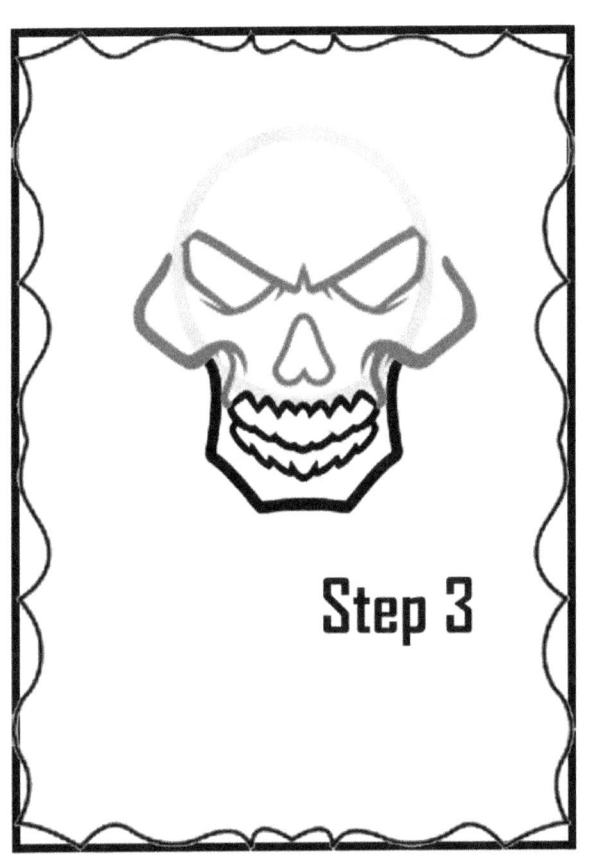

Step 3

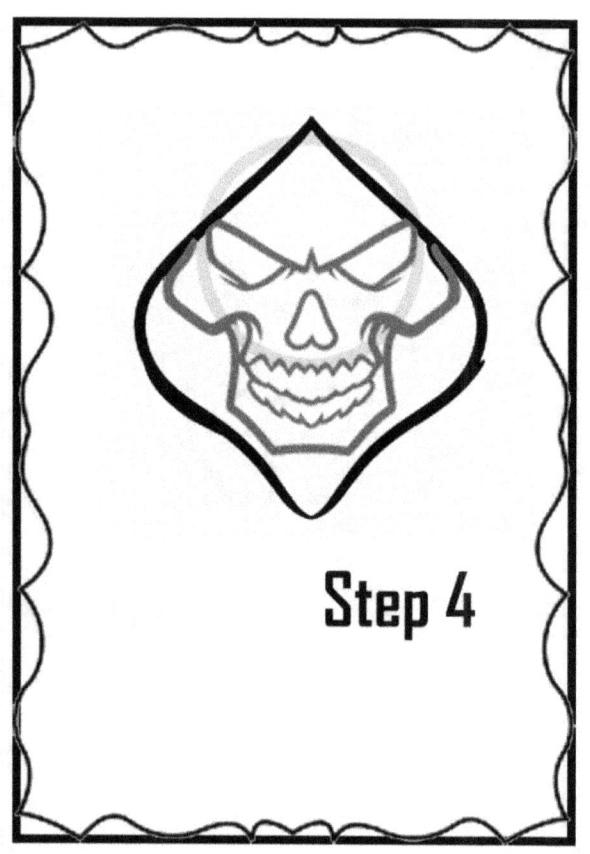

Step 4

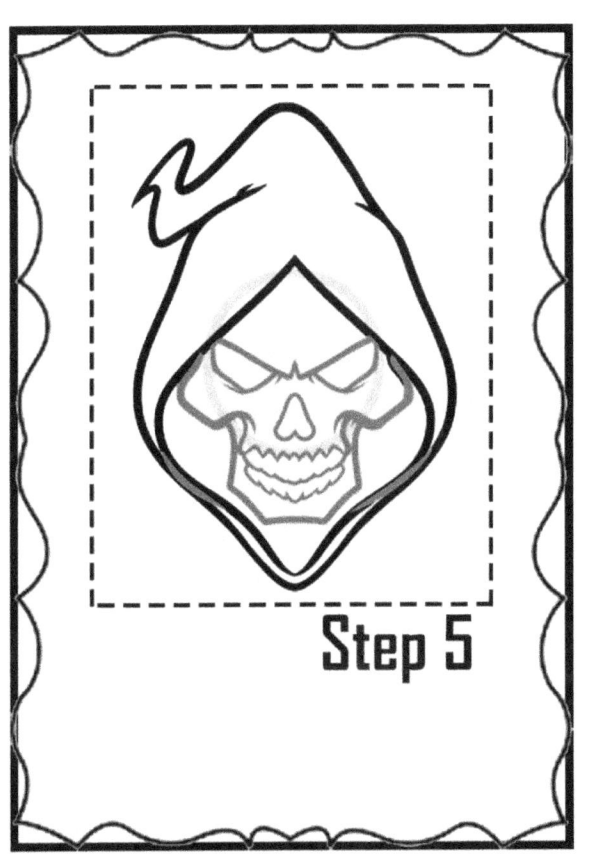

Step 5

Maori Tattoo

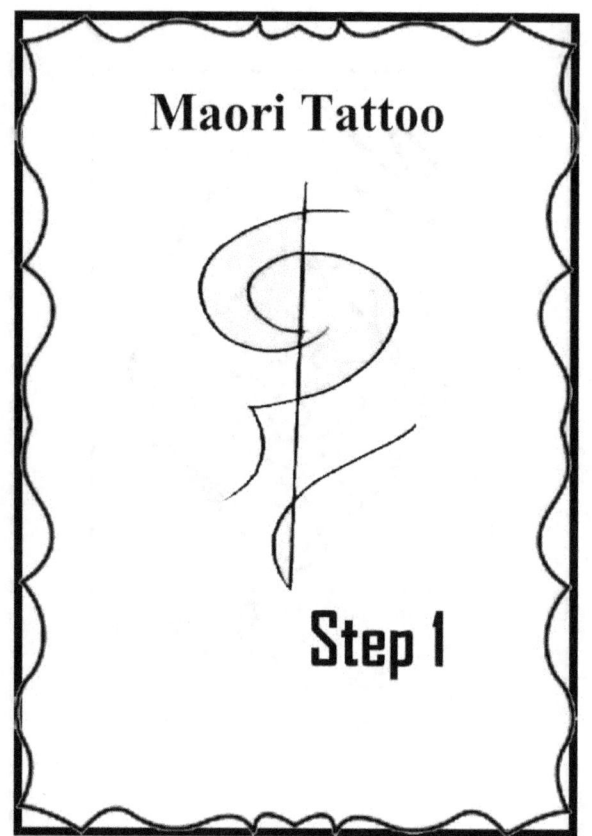

Step 1

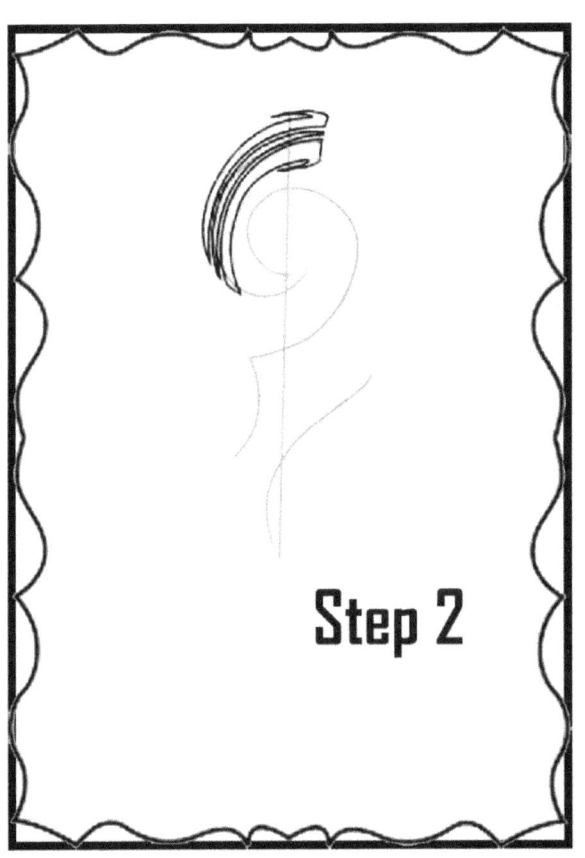

Step 2

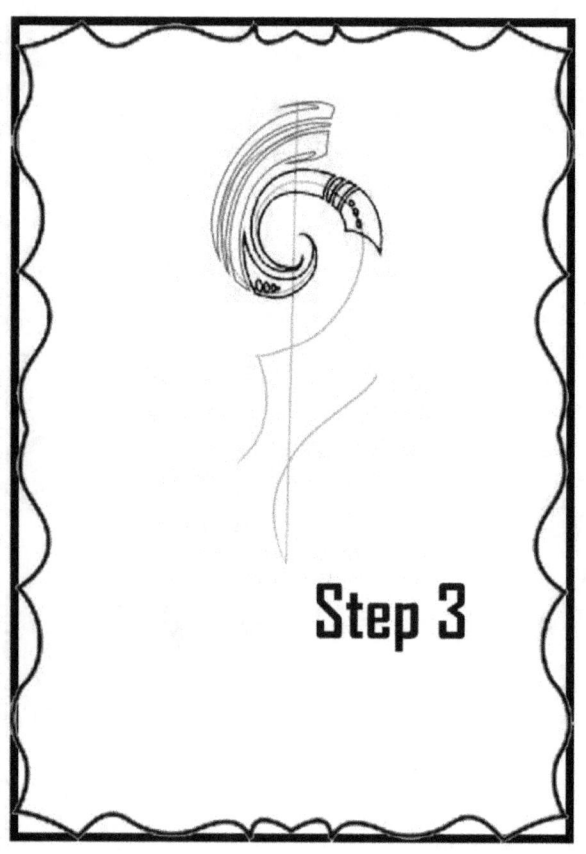

Step 3

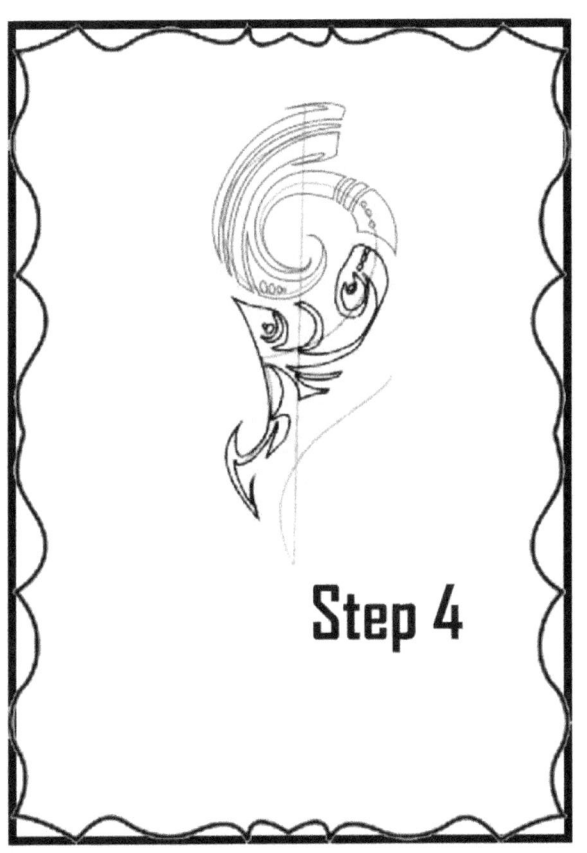

Step 4

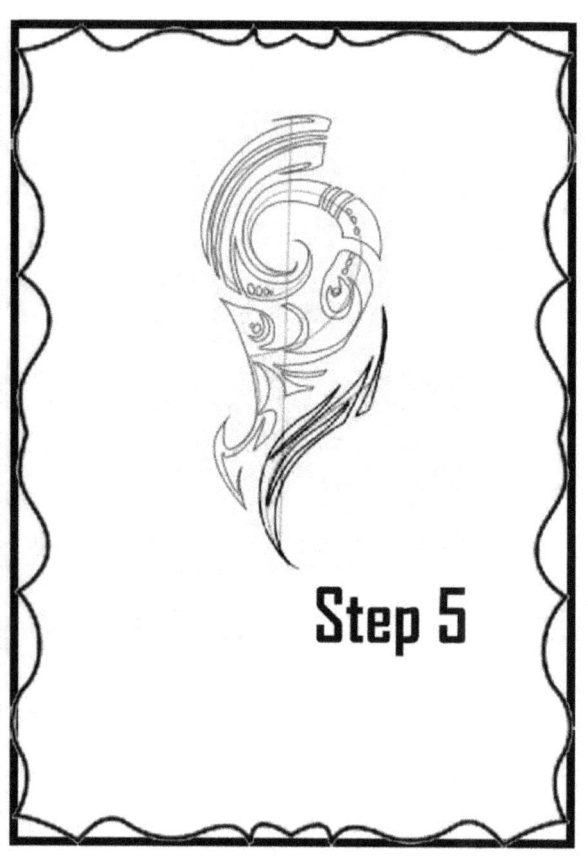

Step 5

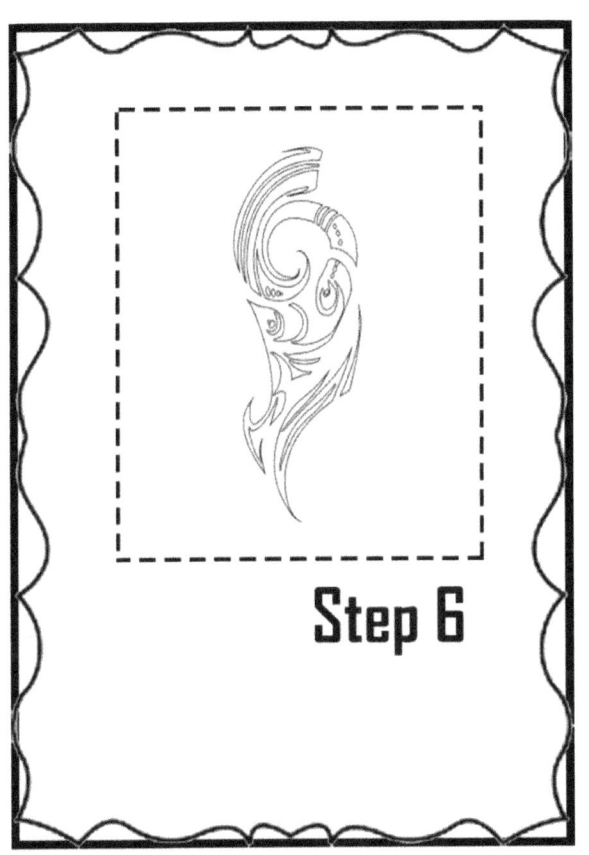

Step 6

Panther Tattoo

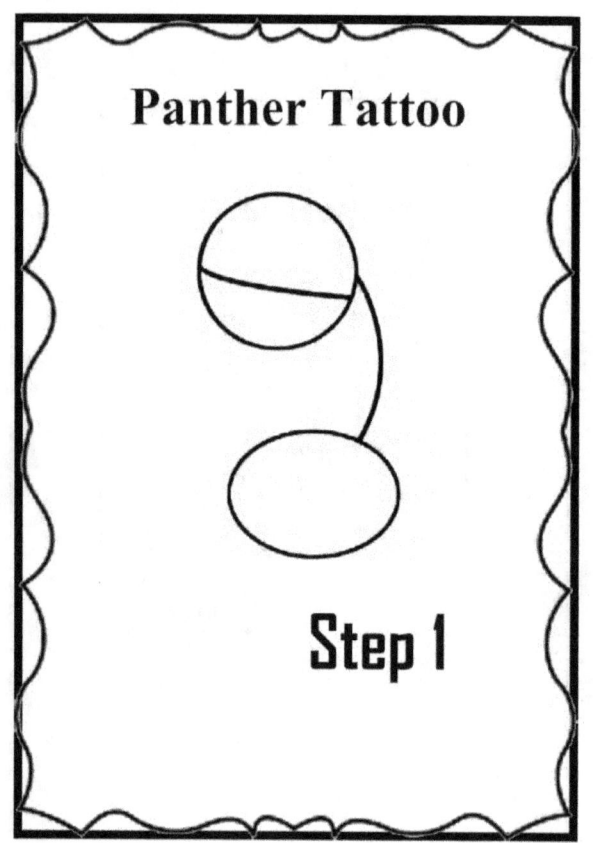

Step 1

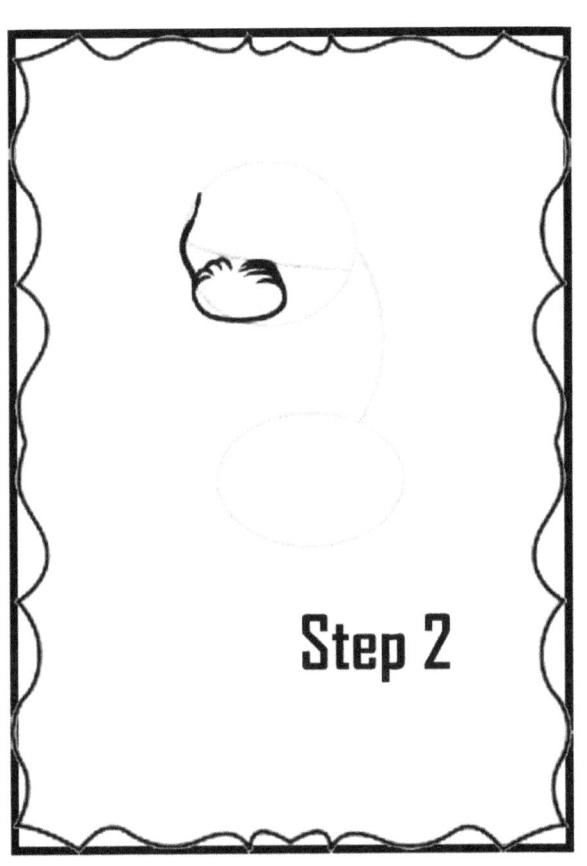

Step 2

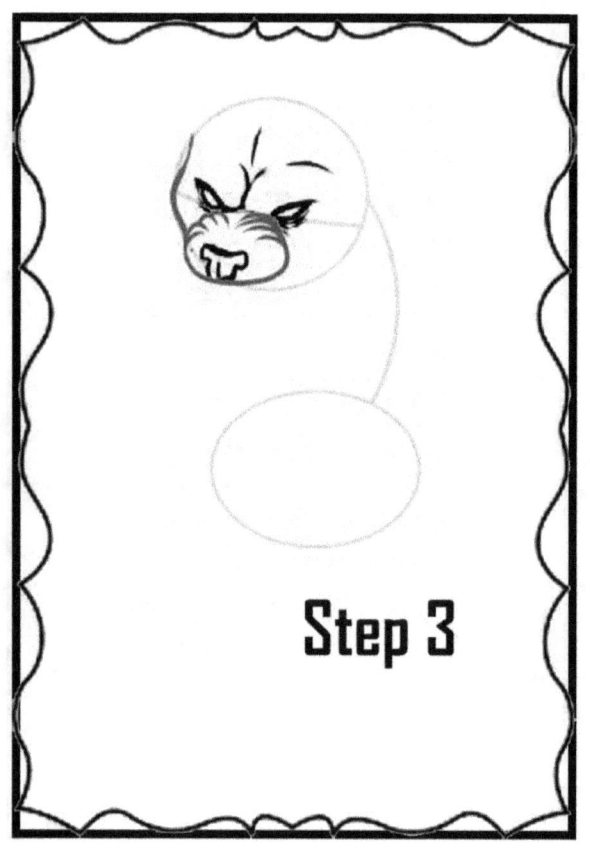

Step 3

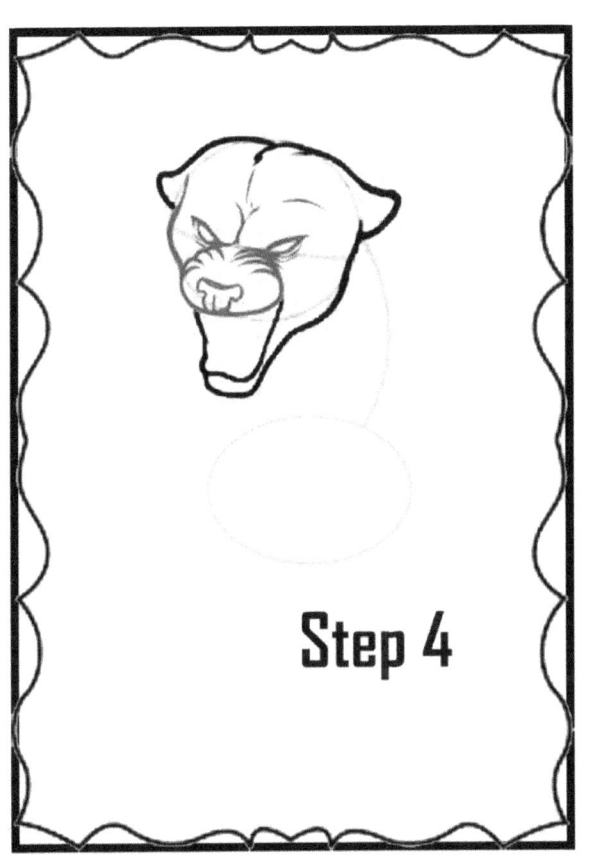

Step 4

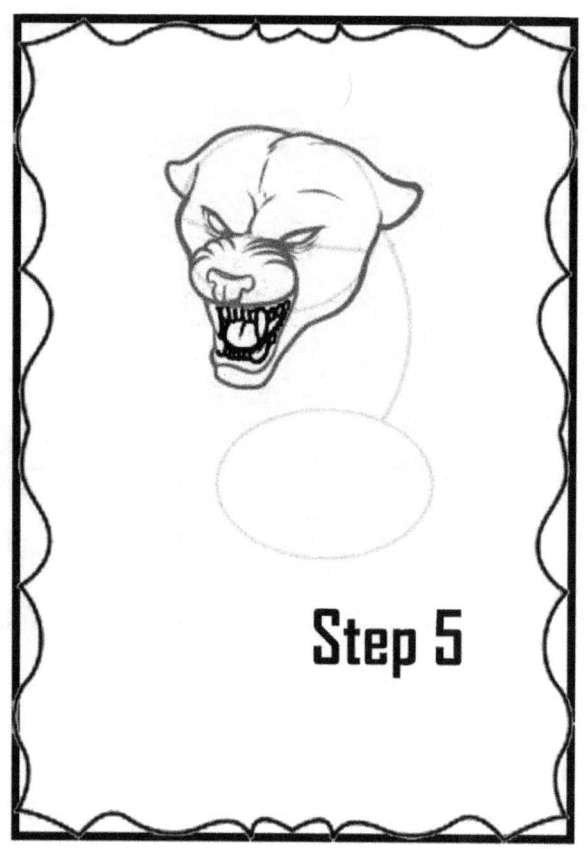

Step 5

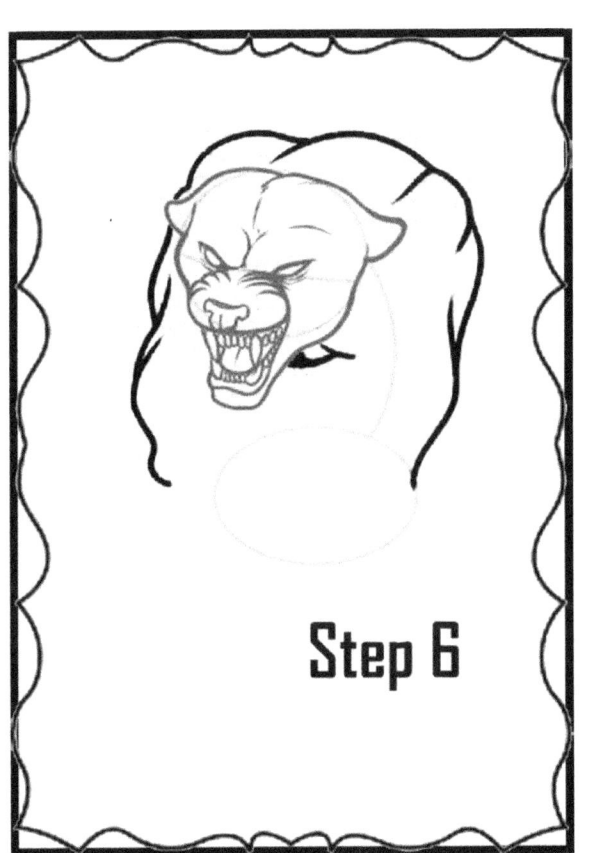

Step 6

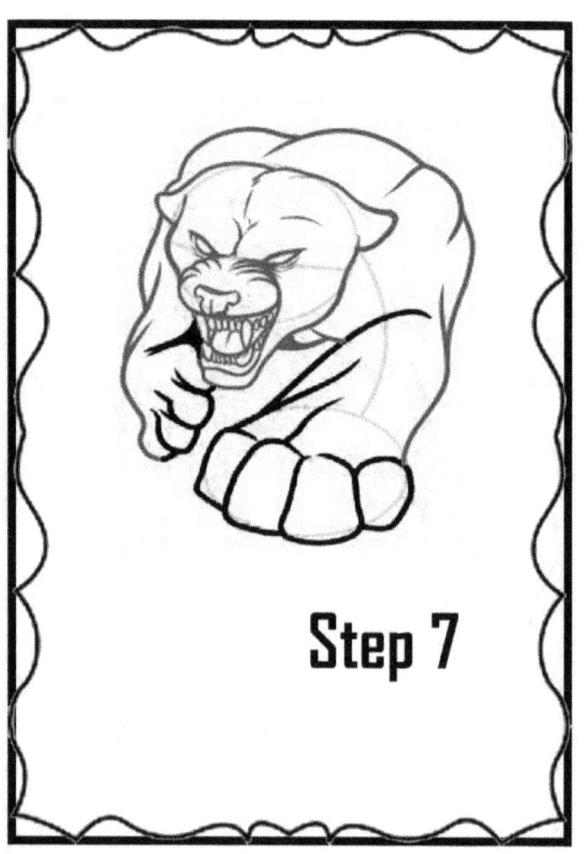

Step 7

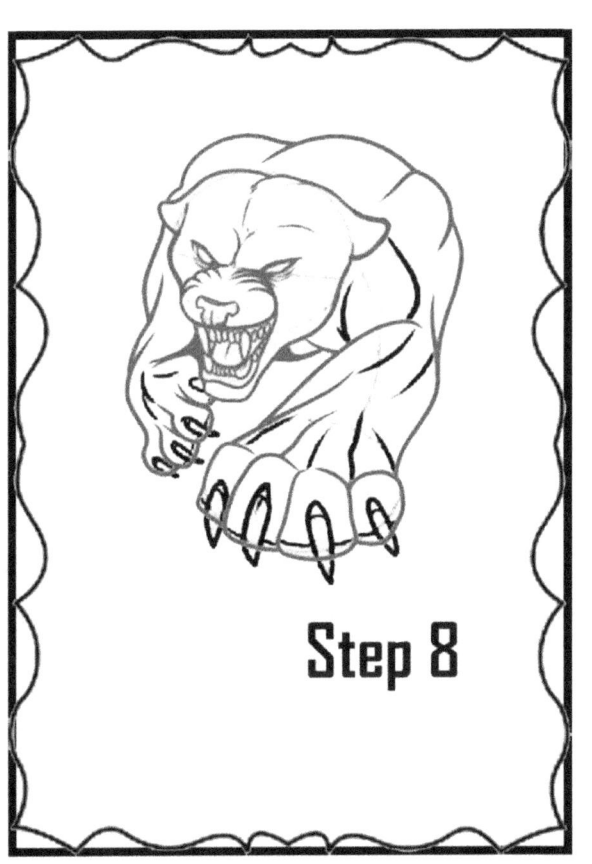

Step 8

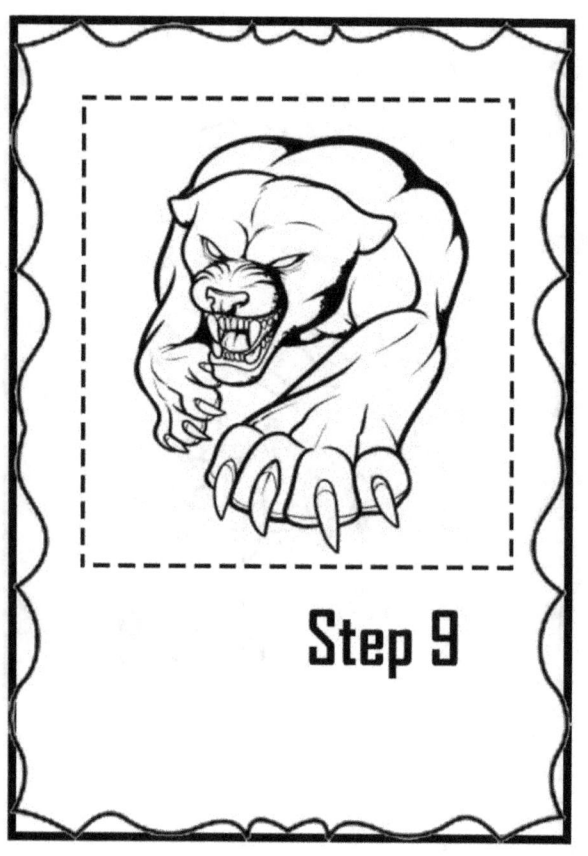

Step 9

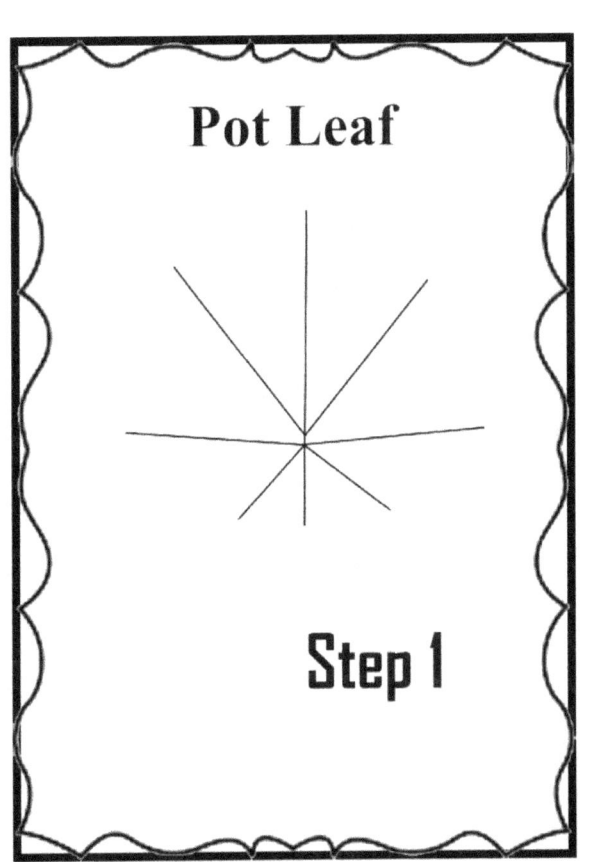

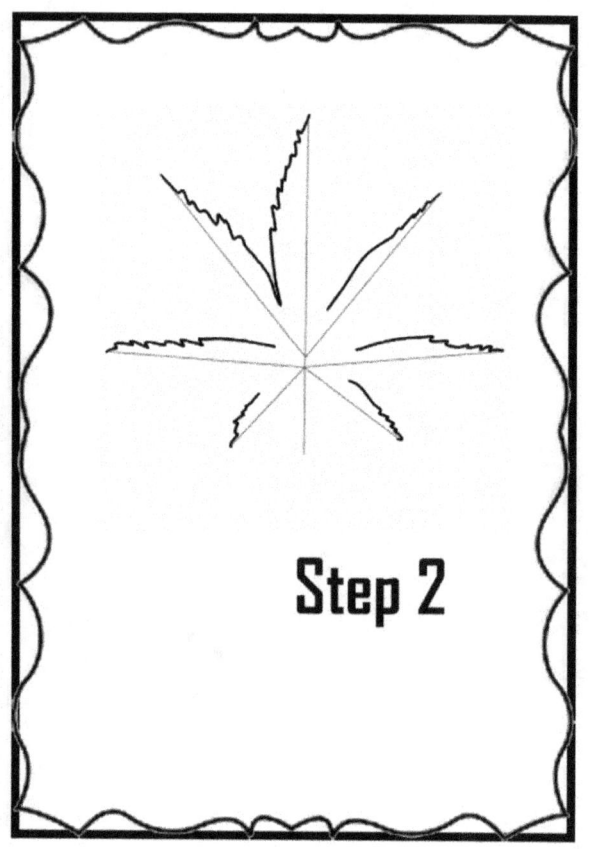

Step 2

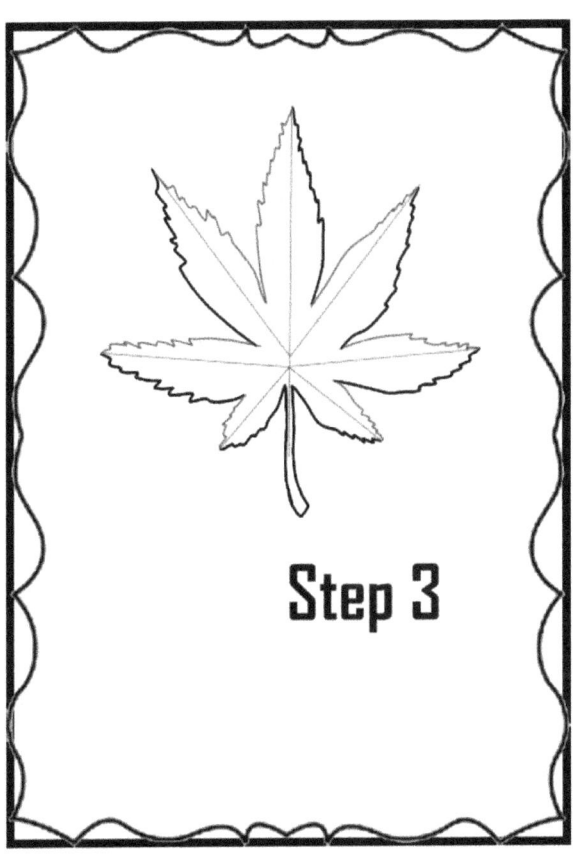

Step 3

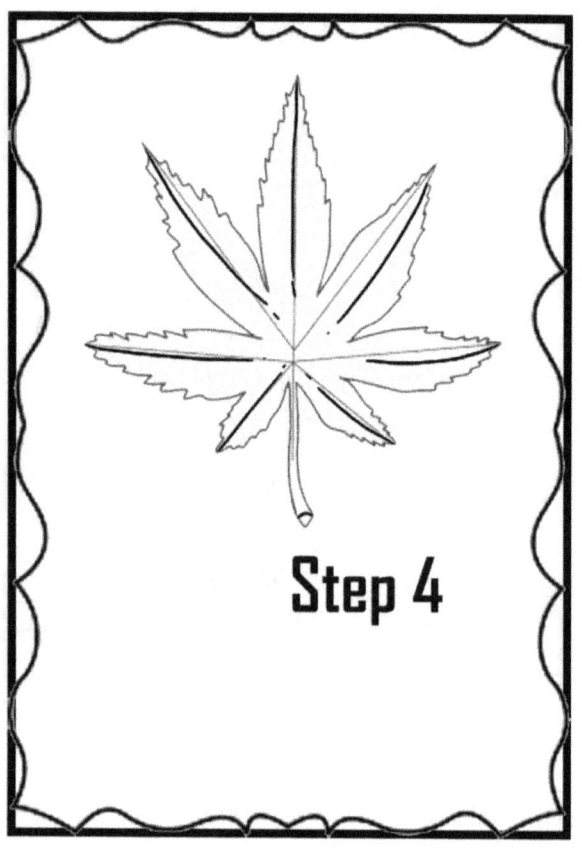

Step 4

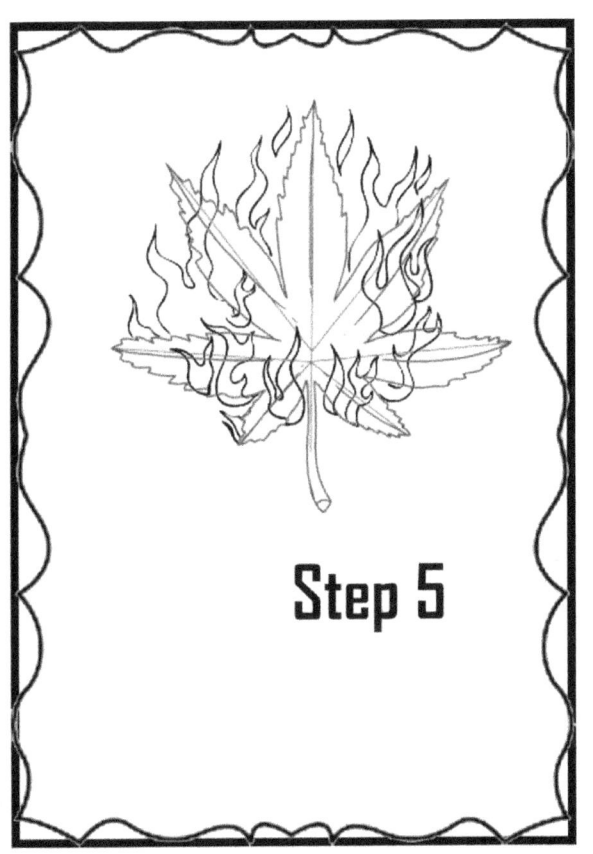

Step 5

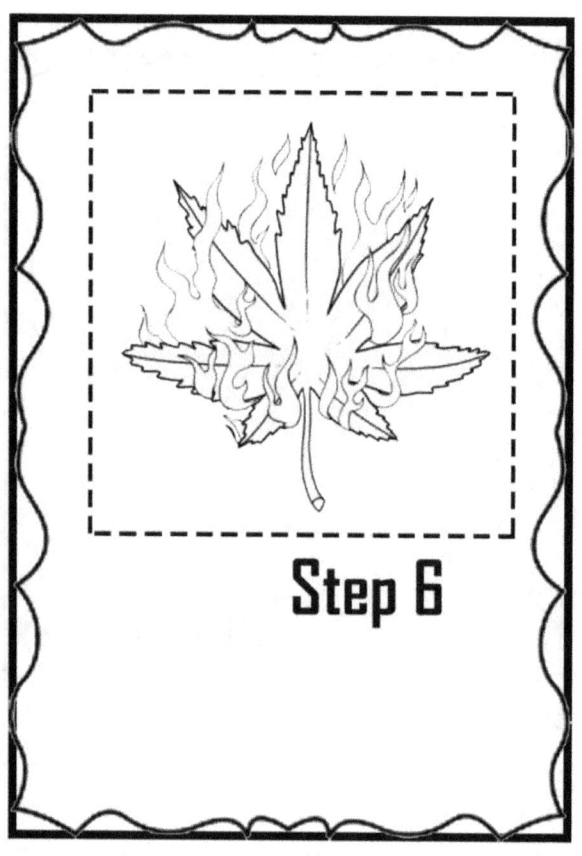

Step 6

Skull on Fire

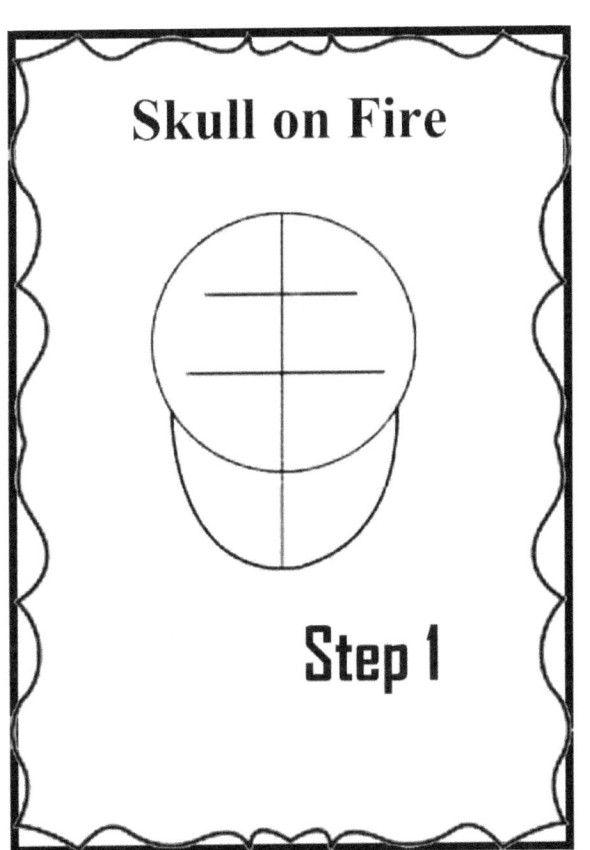

Step 1

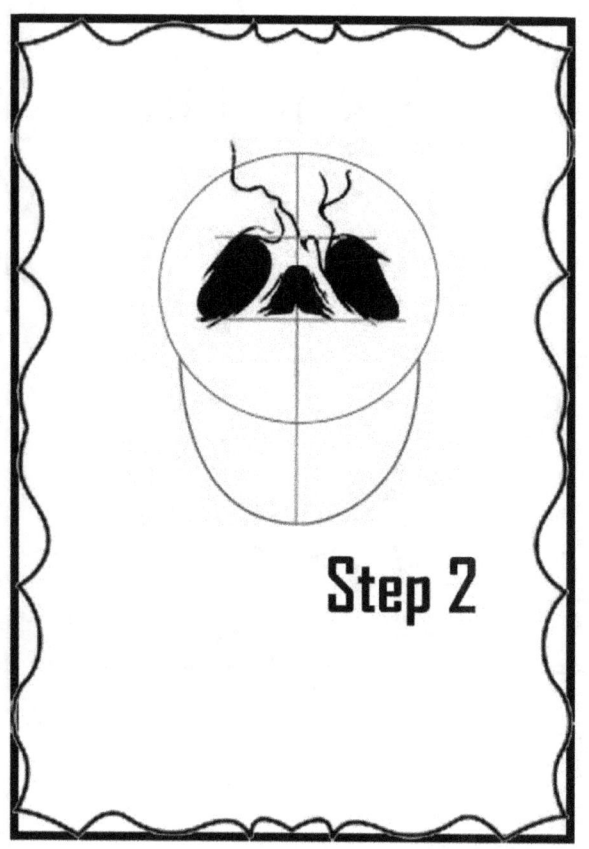

Step 2

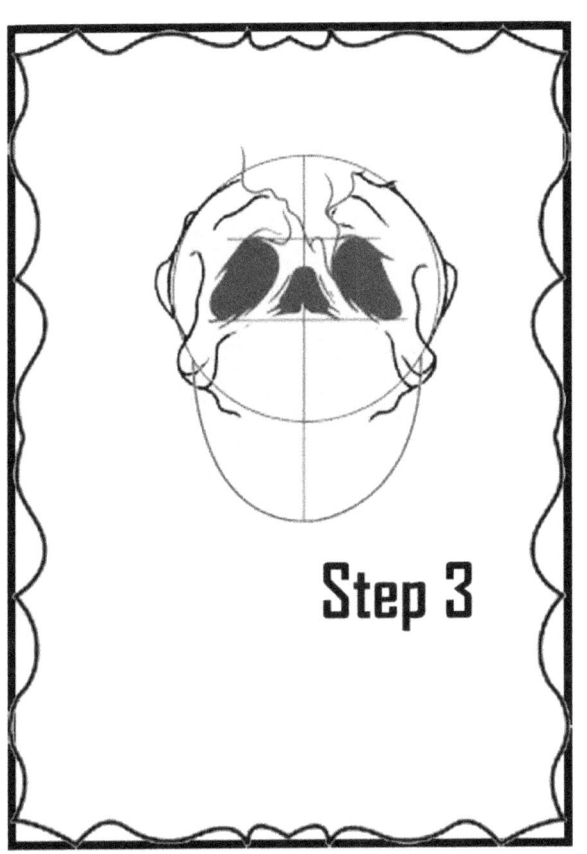

Step 3

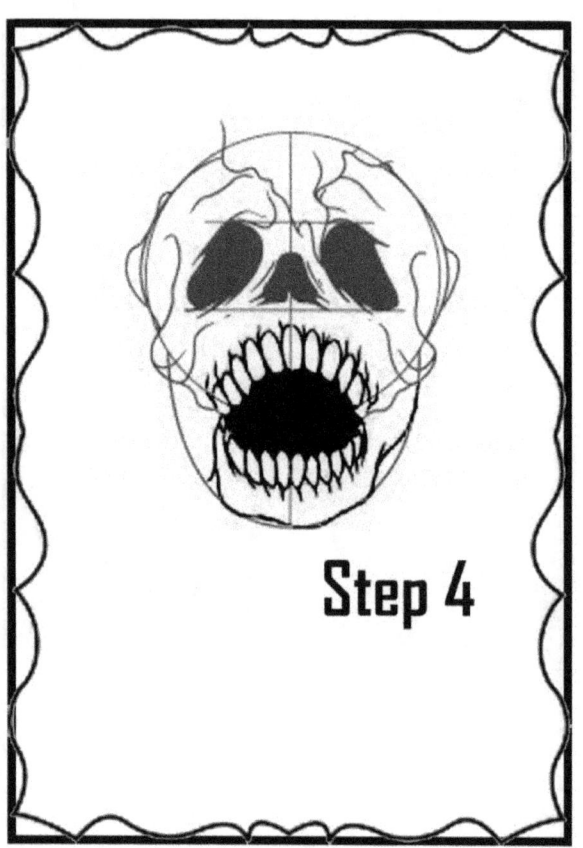

Step 4

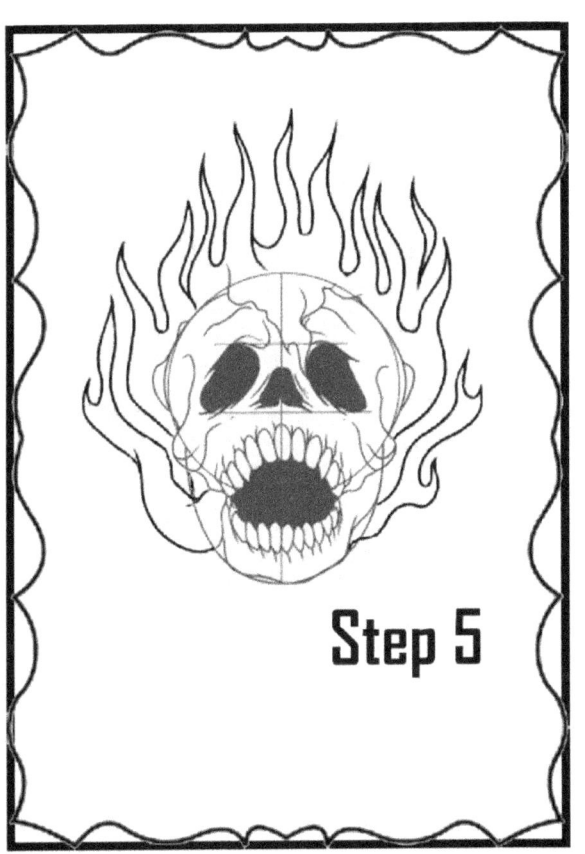

Step 5

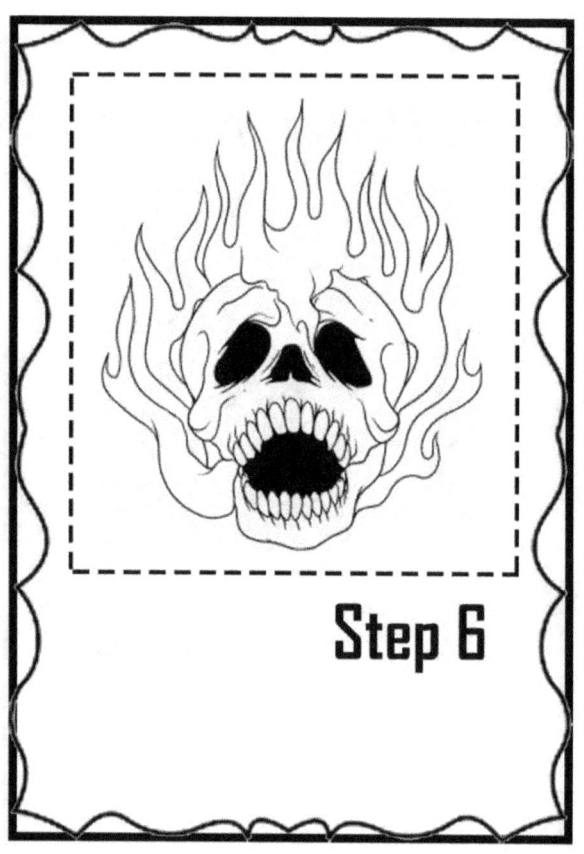

Step 6

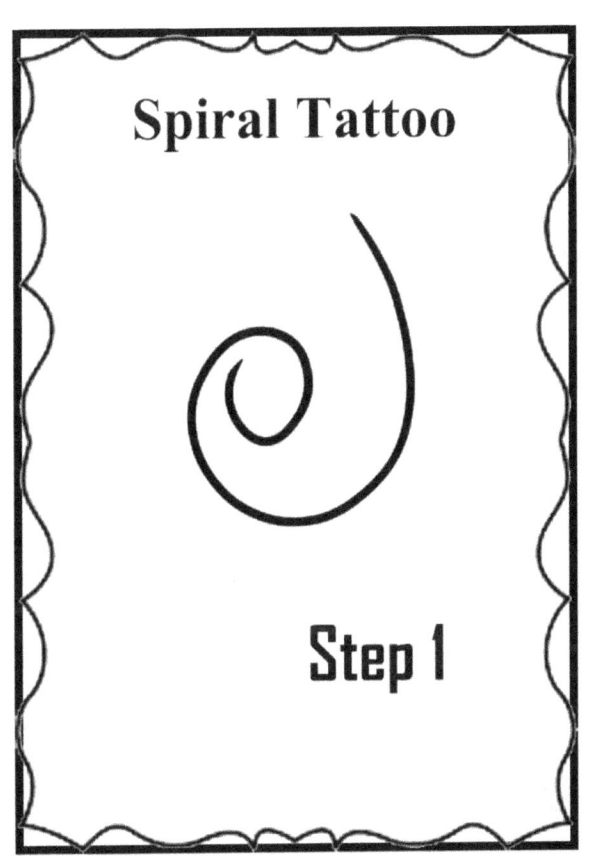

Spiral Tattoo

Step 1

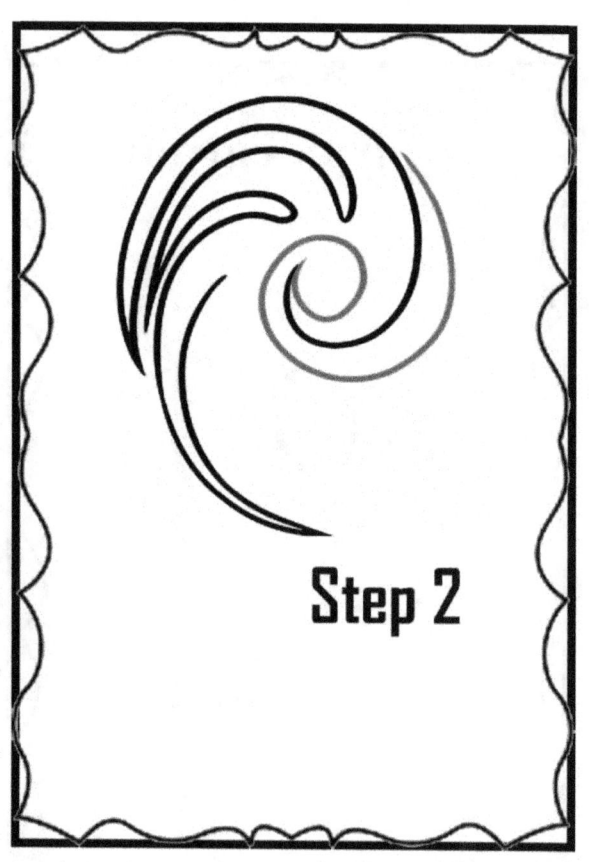

Step 2

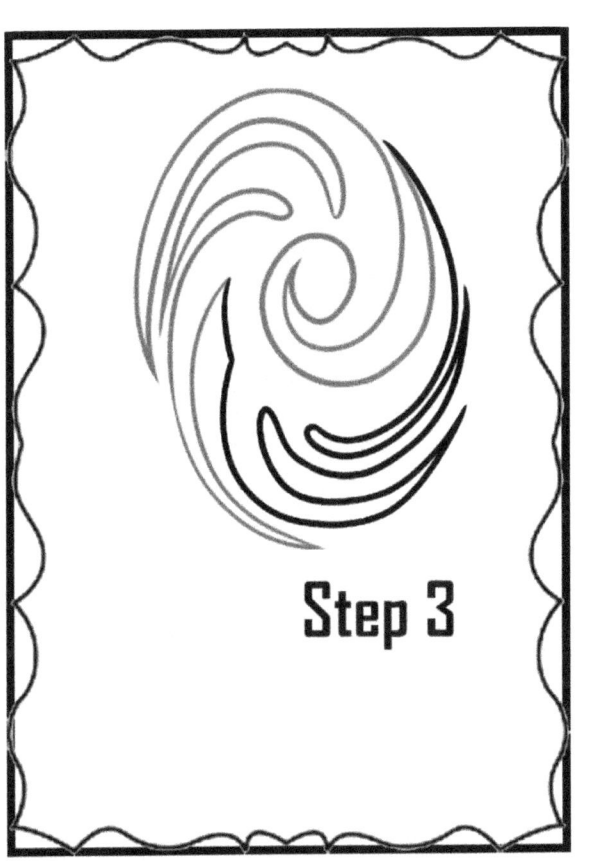

Step 3

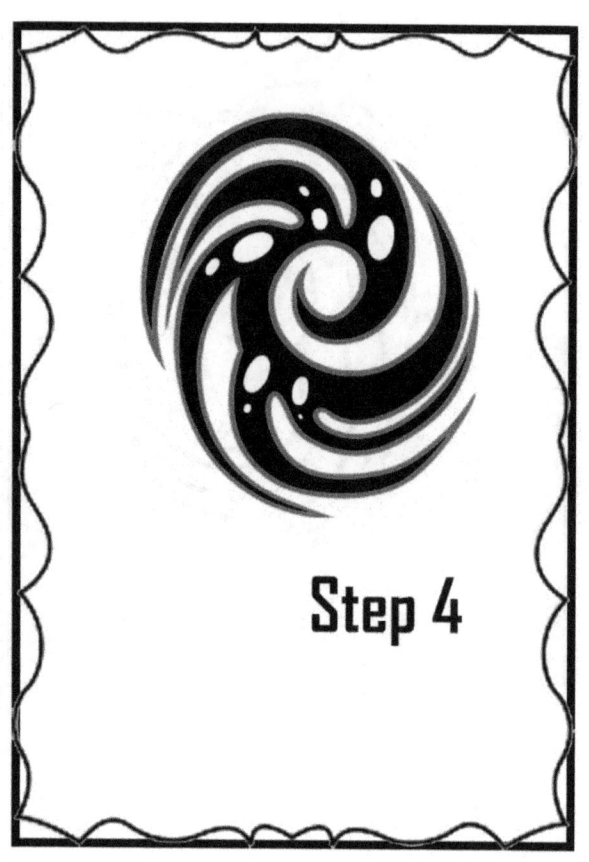

Step 4

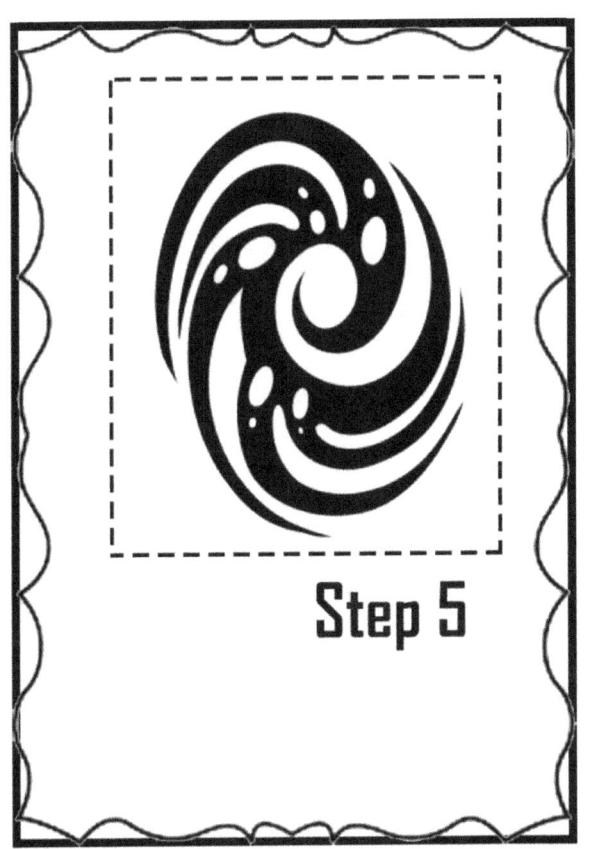

Step 5

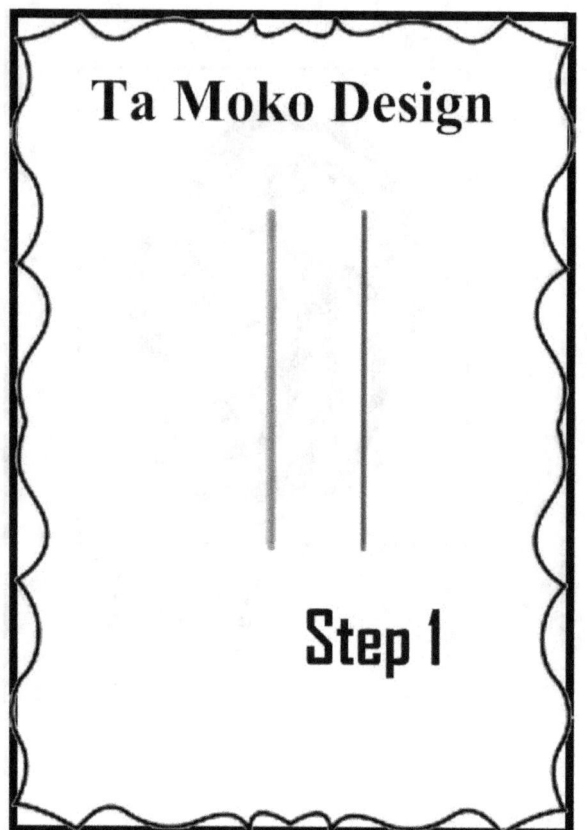

Ta Moko Design

Step 1

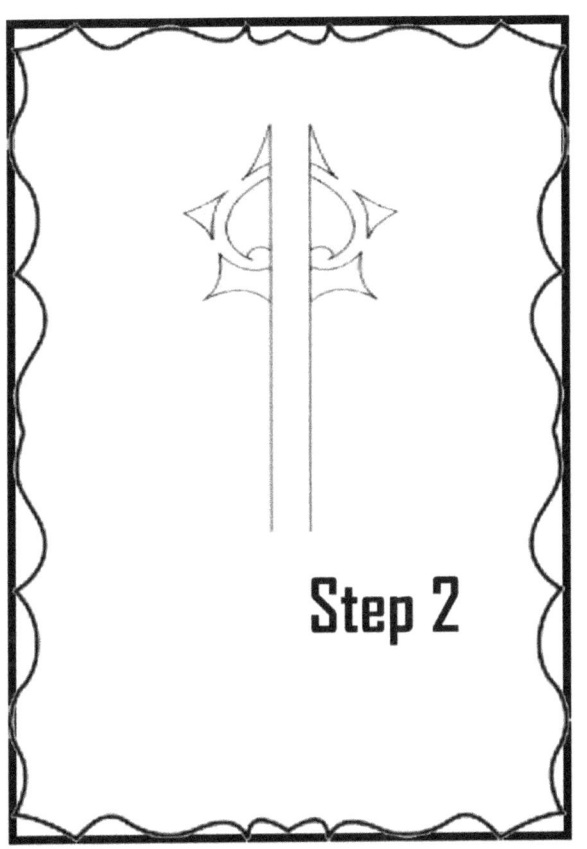

Step 2

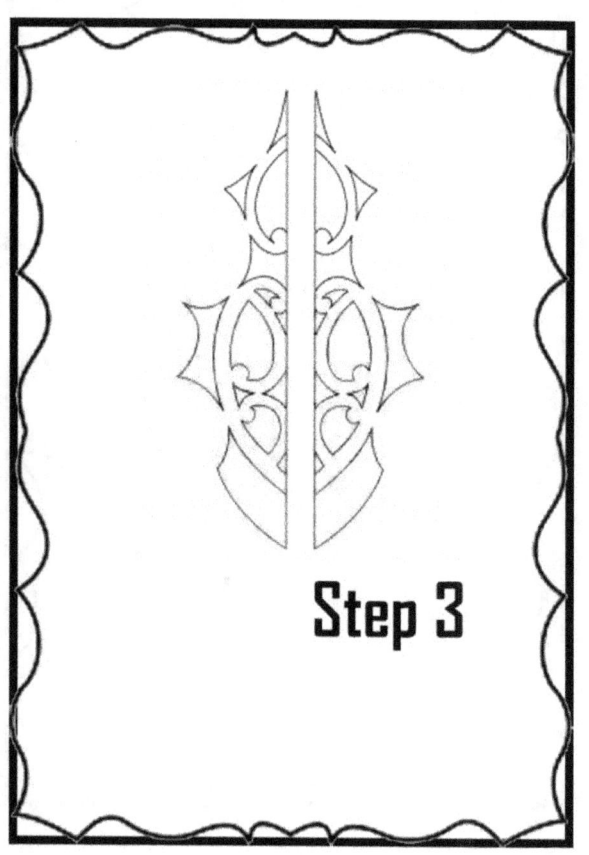

Step 3

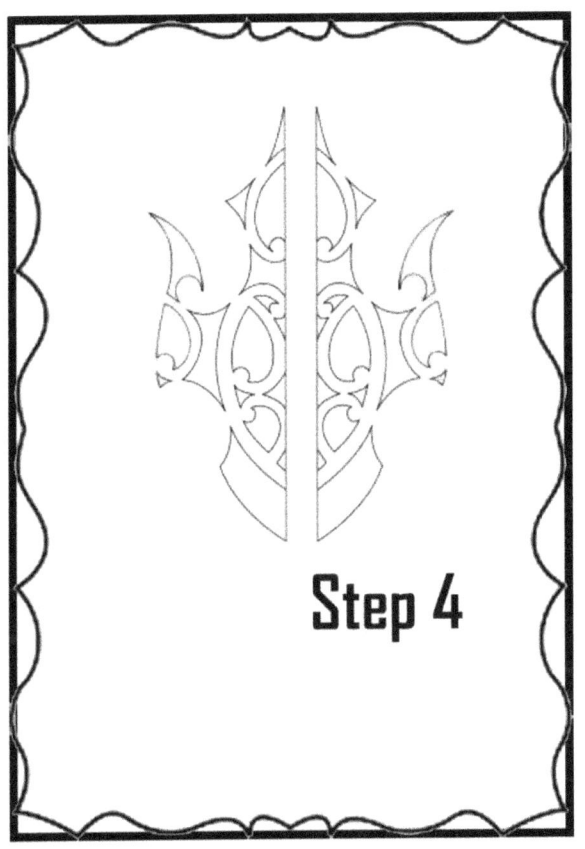

Step 4

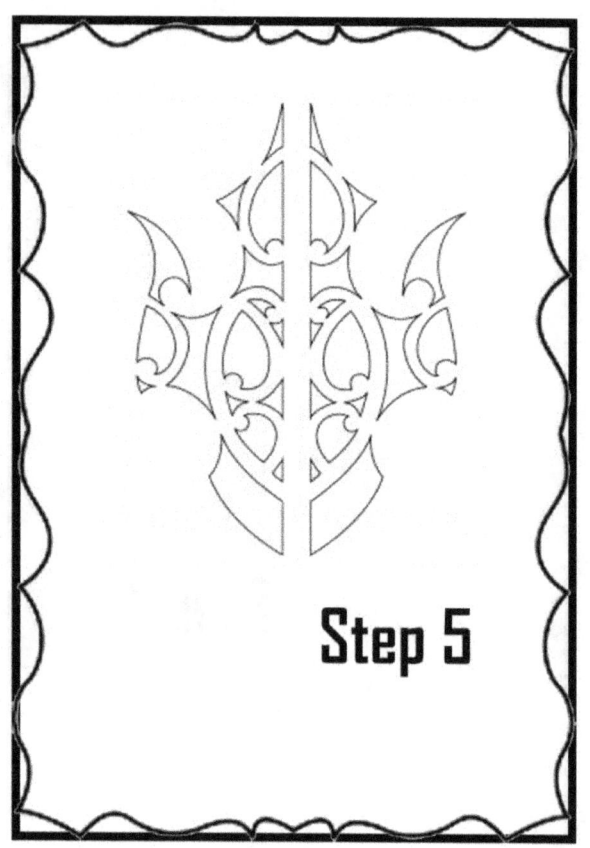

Step 5

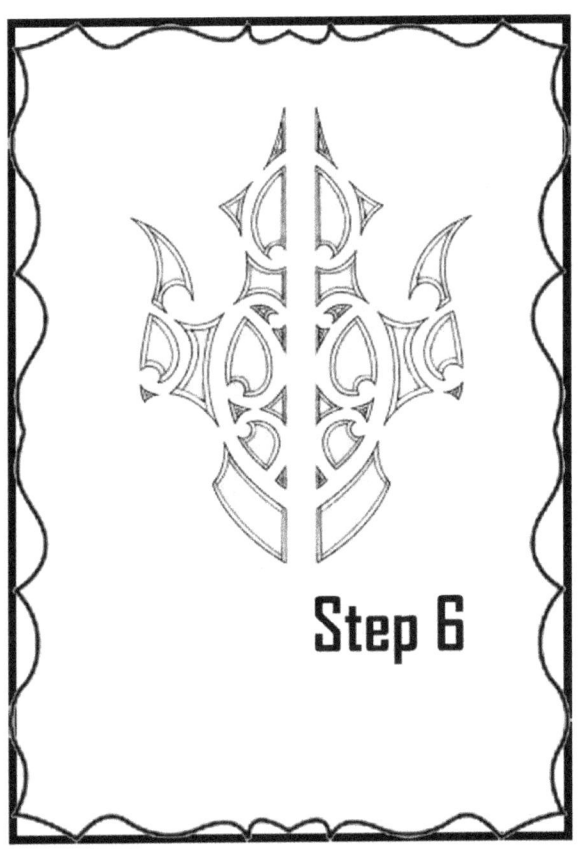

Step 6

Step 7

Tribal Flames

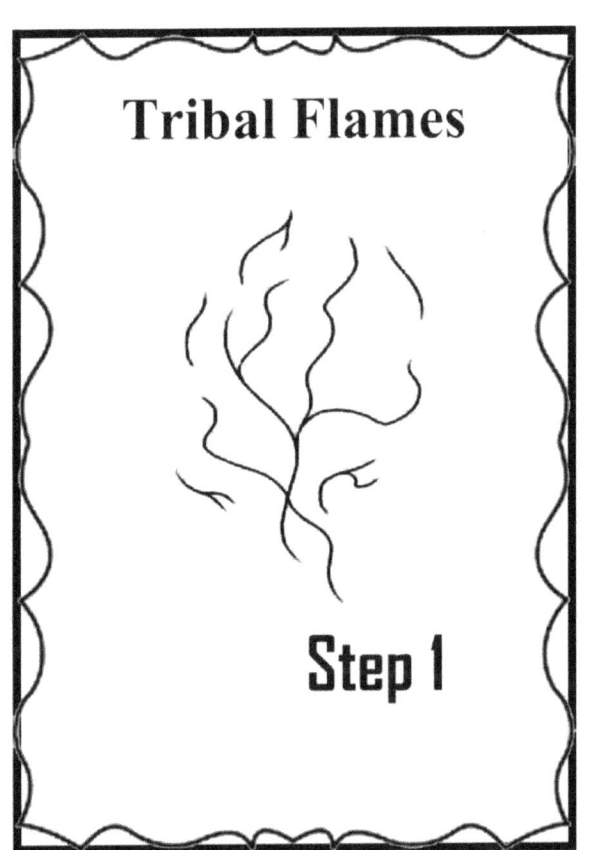

Step 1

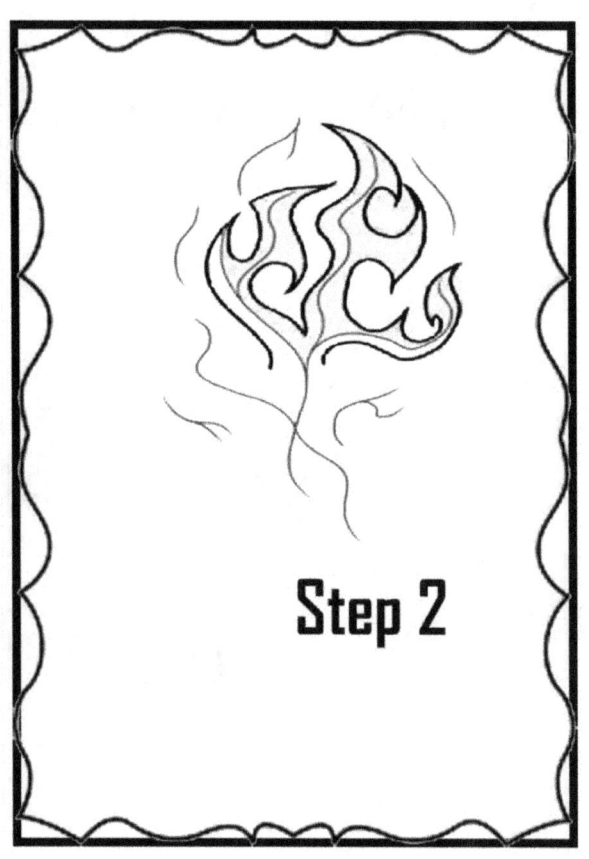

Step 2

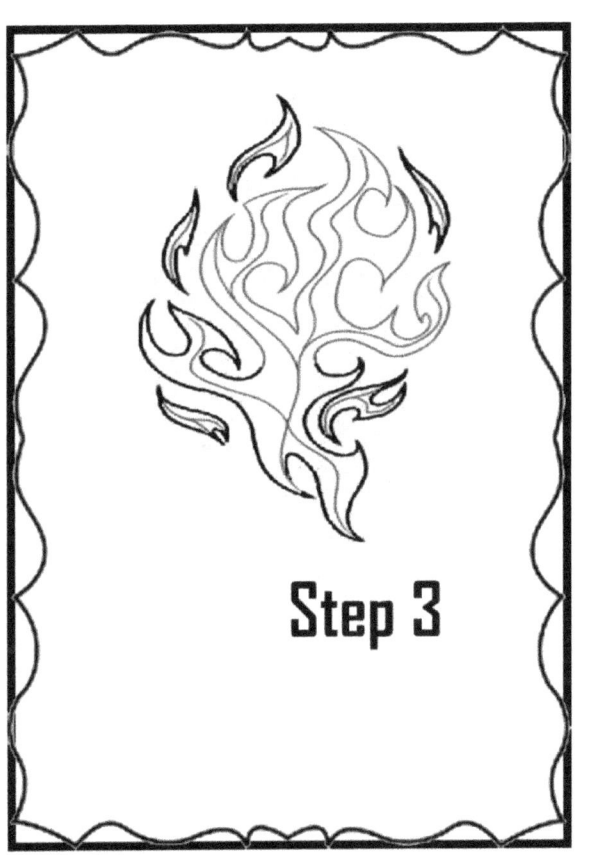

Step 3

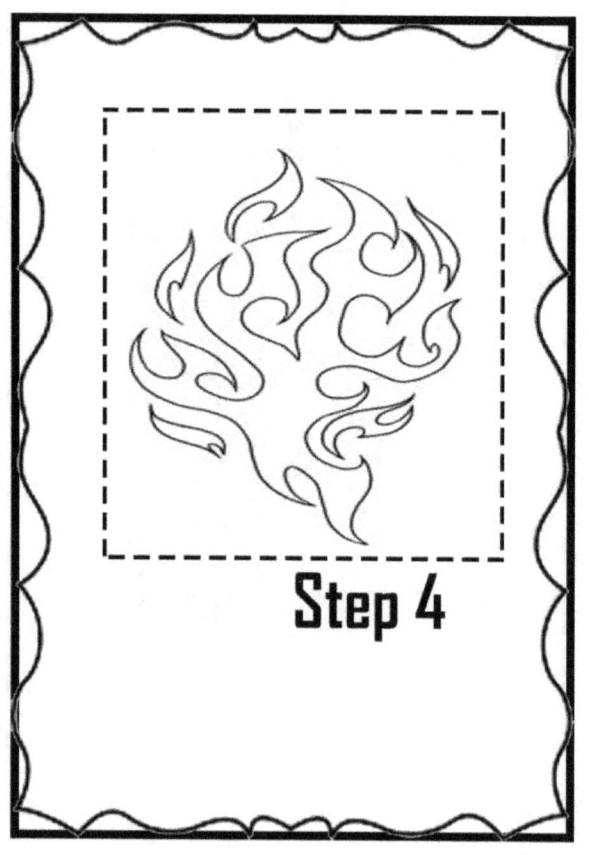

Step 4